RƏQƏMLƏR HAQQINDA HEKAYƏ

THE NUMBER STORY

SMALL BOOK ONE

ENGLISH - AZERBAIJANI

*Numbers Teach Children
Their Number Names*

written and illustrated by

MISS ANNA

Early Reader Edition of *The Number Story 1*
Bronze Medal Winner, 2016 Wishing Shelf Book Award

Library of Congress Control Number: 2018902040

Names: Miss Anna, author.
Title: Number story : numbers teach children their number names / Miss Anna.
Description: Portland, OR: Lumpy Publishing, 2018.
Identifiers: ISBN 978-1-945977-65-7 | LCCN 2018902040
Summary: The pictures and rhymes present stories which introduce numbers 0-10.
Subjects: LCSH Numeration—English--Azerbaijani--Pictorial works--Juvenile literature. | BISAC JUVENILE NONFICTION /
Languages: English--Azerbaijani
Classification: LCC QA141.3 .M57 2018 | DDC 513—dc23

Publisher: Lumpy Publishing
Website: www.missannabooks.com
Email: missanna@missannabooks.com

Paperback: ISBN 978-1-945977-65-7
Printed in the U.S.A.   1 3 5 7 9 10 8 6 4 2

Rəqəmlərin adlarını öyrənmək istəyirsən?

It is very easy and a lot of fun!

Bu çox asan və maraqlıdır!

Say-along our little jingle

Bu mahnını bizimlə birlikdə oxu!

starting from Number One!

Gəl Birinci Rəqəmdən başlayaq!

ONE looks like my one finger.

BİR

mənim barmağıma bənzəyir.

ONE!
BİR!

2

TWO   trails a tail.

İKİnin

quyruğu var.

A TAIL! QUYRUĞU!

3

THREE   has bumps.

ÜÇ

dağlara bənzəyir.

Yaşıl dağlara bir bax!

4

FOUR   carries a sail.

DÖRD

yelkənli qayıqdır.

A SAIL!
YELKƏNLİ QAYIQ!

5

FIVE   is a racing track.

BEŞ

yarış yoluna bənzəyir.

VROOM
VRUMM!

6

SIX curves like a snail.

ALTI

ilbiz kimi bükülür.

A SNAIL! İLBİZ!

7
SEVEN has a sharp angle.
YEDDİ
onun iti küncü var.

OUCH!
UF!

EIGHT is rollercoaster rails.

SƏKKİZ

"Amerika təpələri" attraksionudur.

URA!
YIPPEE!

NINE   is a bubble on a stick.

DOQQUZ

çubuğun ucunda sabun köpüyüdür.

A BUBBLE! SABUN KÖPÜYÜ!

10
TEN   is an eye of a whale.
ON
balinanın bir gözüdür.

HELLO!
SALAM!

And
Və

0

ZERO   is an empty pail.

SIFIR
boş bir vedrədir.

IT'S
EMPTY!
O boşdur!

Thank you for playing with us today.

We had a lot of fun too!

Bu gün bizimlə oynadığın
üçün Sənə təşəkkür edirik.
Bu gün biz çox əyləndik!

We are your Number friends,
Zero to Ten,
Who will be here for you~
Biz sənin Rəqəm dostlarınıq
Sıfırdan Ona kimi!
Biz həmişə burada,
sənin yanında olacağıq~

Bye-bye now!
See you again soon!
Hələlik!
Tezliklə görüşənədək!

The Numbers are *SINGING* too!

To sing-a-long, look for Miss Anna Number Story
at your favorite music store like iTUNES.

MP3

Numbers 0-10
IDENTIFYING & COUNTING

Numbers 11-20
& Ordinals
first, second, third...

Numbers 0-100
& Place Values
ones, tens, hundreds...

About Clocks
& Telling Time
hours, minutes, seconds

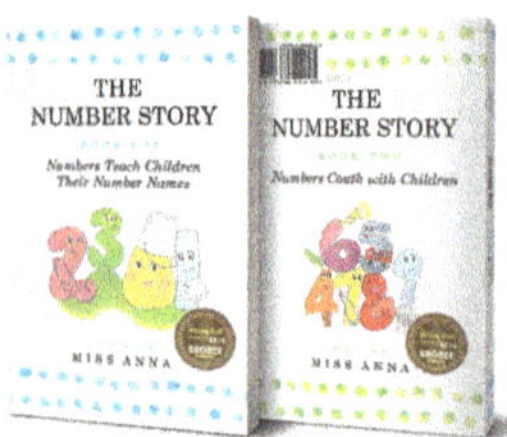

Number Story 1 & 2
isbn: 978-0-996216-48-7

Number Story 3 & 4
isbn: 978-1-945977-01-5

Number Story 5 & 6
isbn: 978-1-945977-06-0

Number Story 7 & 8
isbn: 978-1-949320-40-4

For more Miss Anna books to love,
visit us at

www.missannabooks.com

Numbers are working hard all over the world!
Come Travel the World with Us!

www.ingramcontent.com/pod-product-compliance
Lightning Source LLC
Chambersburg PA
CBHW040859070726
47599CB00035B/2237